We
Work and
Play

by Christopher Rossell

Scott Foresman
is an imprint of

Glenview, Illinois • Boston, Massachusetts • Chandler, Arizona
Upper Saddle River, New Jersey

A horse can work.

A horse can play.

An elephant can work.

An elephant can play.

A dog can work.

A dog can play.

A dog can work and play.